The thoughts outside my head

Claire Hodgetts

BookLeaf Publishing

Presentation by *BookLeaf Publishing*

Web: www.bookleafpub.com

E-mail: info@bookleafpub.com

ISBN: 9789357441995

First edition 2023

This is dedicated to my son Louis and partner Daniel whose love,support and encouragement have been my inspiration.

Happy New Year

May your laughter be plenty
and your dreams all come true
May your health be tip top
Leave the old for the new

May you be surrounded by love
and your purse keeps receiving,
and if things get tough
may you find strength to keep believing

May you achieve all you desire
May your soul fill with cheer
Wishing you all the best
and a Happy New Year

Fair winds and safe harbour

Today we lost a sailor
his final watch is done.
Eight bells have tolled their last
for a husband,father, son.

The day may be tinged with sadness
but forget the sorrow and the woe.
For this is a celebration of the life of an old
Matelot

You took your place on deck
as you sailed across the seas
on the mighty air craft carriers
Bulwark, Ark Royal and Hermes

'Safe in our hands'
the motto you stood by,
as you served your queen and country
following the open seas and sky

No more wakey wakey to the sound of the
reville.
Time for one last muster
before you gently sail away

And over the yardarm
passes the blazing sun.
So now you've crossed the bar
It's time to raise the Pussers rum

So fair winds and safe harbour
Our old oppo, our shipmate
The sea is calling out to you
where your fellow chockheads wait.

An ode to lockdown

When lockdown first began we were filled with
frustration.
There was nothing we could do we were stuck in
isolation,
and it seemed like an eternity
until we could see our friends and family.

We learnt to social distance,
though this was met with some resistance.
While loo rolls and hand wash became rare
commodities.
Face masks became one of the must have
accessories

We looked to the newsreaders for the answers
that we sought.
The weariness on their faces with the updates
that they brought.
But we found our strength, within our
neighbourhood
and we turned the negative into something good.

There were volunteers and helpers, a whiteboard
with daily words of inspiration.
But teaching our kids was a real education.

Numeracy and science and what an earth is a
phonic?
It was a relief to sit down at night with a glass of
gin and tonic!

We picnic'd in the garden for VE day
celebrations
and watched a real live rocket shoot amongst the
constellations.
Captain Tom walked for millions - God bless
him
and Joe wicks endeavoured to keep the nation
trim.

Our homes became our workplace, the school
and the gym.
We crafted and we baked, lots of fun stuff to fit
in
There were rainbows in the windows and we
worried less and less.
For we knew we were in good hands when we
clapped for the NHS.

Our key workers kept us going from
shopkeepers to those in social care.
The burden of responsibility never too much for
them to bare.
People danced in the street, wrote songs and
posted videos for all to see

And the clays had their own naked gardeners
committee

We planted sunflowers and hoped that they
would grow
and stood in endless queues- moving oh so slow!
At time's we didn't bother getting dressed
and we went with the flow - no point in getting
stressed.

We started home improvements thank heavens
for eBay!
No time to rest, lots of jobs to occupy the day.
And we thought how lucky we were to have our
family together
As we tried to get through lockdown without
strangling each other

We were so happy to have WhatsApp, and what
fun we had with Zoom
Just like having your friends and family in your
living room.
We had our daily 30 minutes allocated exercise
but for other activities we learnt to improvise.

It's been a funny time if you know what I mean
The experiences we've had, the things we've
seen
But we are thankful we get to see another day.

And hopefully the lessons we've learnt will be here to stay

If I had a wish

If I had a wish to live someone elses life for a
day
I'd choose to be Kristy in each and every way.

Id walk into the office with a cheery grin on my
face
I'd tidy my desk and put everything in it's place

I'd make sure that I had an apple a day
or yoghurt covered nuts as they are also ok

I'd get my work done as I'd be no shirker always
striving to be a great social worker

My hair would be wavy or sometimes straight
but whatever I did it would always look great

My nails would be painted a different colour
each day
my accessories matching my outfit I'd have such
an array

I'd be creative showing off my artistic flair my
poems and drawings or my cooking fare

I'd smuggle under the duvet watching cheesy 80s
flicks
Adventures in babysitting or Labyrinth have all
the best bits.

I'd plan what I'm cooking for my gorgeous
hubby John a quick nip to morrisons before all
the pixzas have gone.

I'd walk my dog and complete my cross training
I'm never defeated even if it is raining.

I'd travel to oz, las Vegas and other far away
places and visit ascot for a day at the races

I'd drink lots of vodka but not with red bull.
Cider mojitos I love em all

I'd restore lots of furniture and make it all
pristine. My house would be decorated all in
green.

If you had a wish just like me
And could be anyone who would you be

Battle of the sexes

If men click their fingers and ask for tea
Stand up and shout equality
Women's lib and burn that bra
The reason women have come so far
It started long ago to quote
When suffragettes did win the vote
For women at last to have a say
on what goes on in the world today

Although men have tried to eliminate
women from the men's world and discriminate
They've laughed they've mocked they've jeered
Women have fought and clapped and cheered

A woman's place isn't in the home
to bring up children all alone
To feed the men who earn the crust
and to be the perfect wife with a double D bust

We're battling through to achieve success
The fairer sex will not be second best
We can turn our hands to anything
and don't grow up wishing for a wedding ring

The men want to keep us in our place

Subordinate and fair of face
But we no longer have to take their shit
Men don't have to agree but they have to lump
it.

Beware

Listen girls beware
There are no nice men just bastards out there
They cause nothing but heartache and pain
Each one says their different but they're all just
the same

They act nice and sweet but they're trying to
trick us
It's all just a ploy to get into our knickers
The way that they treat you makes you feel like
a slag
they don't want commitment they just want a
shag

Their brains are confined within their jeans
they treat women as objects as sexual machines
They don't like it that women are able to think
They'd rather they were chained to the kitchen
sink

I don't think they've ever heard of love
That's easy to see from reading above
All they want is sex sex sex
And when they complain they move onto the
next

How can we get it through to their heads
Women are not objects to be confined to beds
All we ask for is s bit of understanding
Is that unfair or too demanding

So girls just heed this advice
Next time you think a man's bring nice
Make it very clear that women are not fools
If you mess us around you could lose your balls.

Advice to a hen

I'd like to say a few words as we sit upon this
boat.
Before we've drank enough to keep us all afloat.
Getting this party started is definitelythe plan
as we head for fun and frolics in good old for
Amsterdam.
We all know that we're here to celebrate
The last few days of freedom of our kind and
funny mate.
The blushing bride to be doesn't know what we
have planned
Probably best she doesn't or she might jump ship
for land

So here are some tips for a happy married life
that will help you on the way to becoming the
perfect wife.

Keeping his belly full is definitely the trick but if
that's not the way to his heart then you could try
a sharp stick.

Never go to bed mad stay up and fight and never
go to sleep without kissing each other
goodnight.

Never argue about money there's never enough
anyway and never bring up his past mistakes
he'll make new ones the following day.

And if that doesn't work then let's not make it
complex.
Men are simple beings just given him lots of
sex.

So everyone raise your glass to the blushing
bride to be.
Remember her the way she is now, because soon
she'll be drunk and disorderly!
So here is a toast to you my love on your
wonderful Hen weekend.
You are a very special person, we each thank
you for being our friend.

Goodbye to working life Mrs Dawson

Finally the time has come to say goodbye to
working life
More time to spend with family as Grandma,
Mother, Wife

You've made it through got out alive
Now there's no more nine till five

You've worked your way from home help to
adult social care
Supporting those in need to sorting homes in
disrepair
You'll try anything once you'll give it a whirl
And was once the office pin up girl

Back and forwards to the hospital wards
No time then to ever get bored
Seconded to the district where you've been for a
while
With your north east charm and a dazzling smile

You'll get stuck in you'll do what it takes
Except wild animals especially snakes

It's been stressful, eventful at times it's been
trippy
But you've been able to tackle anything once
you've put on your lippy

No more verbal abuse so put away your flak
jacket
More time for merry making by reuniting hinge
and bracket
No more allocations too many cases to pick
Instead there's more time to spend with your
Mick

No more Wednesday panel to fill you with dread
No more working out budgets that hurt your
head
No more duty or answering phones
More time now to show off your cheekbones

No more assessments, care planning or reviews
Time to hang up that laptop and go shopping for
shoes
No more working to deadlines tick tock tick tock
And anytime now is gin o'clock

You'll leave a big gap and although they'll
recruit
There's no-one else who could fill your boots
So happy retirement Mrs Dawson
Your future is bright it's gonna be awesome

What is that smell ?

What the hell
is that smell
Has something died?

It's behind the chaise long
and it really does pong
And the smell will not subside

I have to investigate
before I hyperventilate
And get the thing outside

Get the broom
Clear the room
Everyone step aside

I can seen it now
Holy cow
It smells like formaldehyde

What is the culprit
Arising from the cess pit
I hope it's not still alive

It's black and furry

And full of debris
'That's my sock' my husband cried!

For Daddy

I'm glad you are my daddy
and that I'm your son
Because when we are together
We always have great fun

We'll play games as you bounce me on your
knee
And before I go to sleep you will read to me

You'll hold me in the air and play rockets in the
sky
And sit me on your shoulders so I can see up
high

You'll be there when I cry and help me to be
strong
And when I get my toys out you will play along

You'll take me lots of places and we'll take
mummy too
You'll teach me to try my best at all the things I
do

You'll show me how to leave, my socks upon
the floor

Your jokes and silly faces will make me laugh
for evermore

You'll teach me DIY and how to fix a car and
one day I hope to be as clever as you are

And when I am a man I hope that I can be as
good a Dad to my kids as you have been to me.

My Grandparents

Grandparents are all things great
Like cuddles and kisses and staying up late
Like presents and sweets and having fun
Like snug winter nights and summer days in the
sun

You'll love me and lead me and show me the
way
You'll nurture me,comfort me, wipe my tears
away
I know you'll be with me wherever I roam
Watching over me always until I'm safely home

You'll show me the difference between right and
wrong
And fill my world with laughter and song
Tell me stories about yesteryear
And teach me about family who are no longer
here

You'll show an interest in all that I choose
From riding a bike to my first pair of shoes
I'll always be happy and never be blue
As I'm so lucky to have grandparents like you.

A day at the zoo

Let's go to the zoo cmon everyone
There's lots to explore it will be such fun
Pack up your bag it could be a long day
Snacks and some drinks will keep hunger at bay
If everyone's ready let's go what a treat
Now what will we see and who will we meet

I am a lion king of the pride
A hunter by nature I take it all in my stride
A swish of my tail and my majestic mane
Tracking my prey is my favourite game
With a flash of my teeth and a flick of my paw
The last thing you'll here is my almighty roar

I am a sss..nake and I live in a nest
My bite could be deadly as my fangs suggest
I slither on my belly looking for prey
My forked tongue helps me smell and shows me
the way
I am a charmer look into my eyes
A hiss or a rattle will give away my surprise

I am an elephant part of a herd
My ears are so big they can hear every word
I'm the biggest animal on land

And I can easily sleep where I stand
My trunk is my weapon, my hose and my
trumpet
I am very clever and I never forget.

I am a giraffe I tower above
With my long neck and legs I can reach the
tallest leaves that I love
I have a patterned coat and what look like horns
on my head
The lion is my enemy from whom I fear
And Africa was my home before I came here

I am a penguin I love swimming and diving
With a waddle here and there you can see me
arriving.
My black and white coat keeps me safe and
looks smart
I make catching fish a true work of art
My home is Antarctica I love ice and snow
And everyone loves us to put on a show.

The zoo is now closing its time to leave
But come come back again there's lots more to
see

Gorillas and buffalo's, cheetahs and meerkats as
well
Come and see us we all have a story to tell

Leopards and rhinos we are here too
As well as parrot and spiders, and a white
cockatoo
So we must say goodbye with a squawk, roar,
hiss, twit twoo
We hope you've enjoyed, your day at the zoo.

I love you forever

I loved you first when I felt your heartbeat
I loved you more when I saw your tiny feet
I loved you again when you looked into my eyes
I loved you when I sang you lullabys
I loved you further when you first smiled at me
I loved you deeper when you giggled with glee
I loved you truly when you held my hand
I loved you my son when you tried to stand
And I will love you always for completing our family
And I'll love you forever and ever eternally

A fairytale for adults

Long ago in the lane of Oz
A princess cried and all because
The man she loved had been cast under a spell
by wicked witch Leanne Queen bitch from hell

Let's go back to where the story starts
of throbbing loins and pumping hearts
Princess Joanne from the Kingdom of Brum
Sat wishing that someday her Prince Charming
would come .

Prince Perry our hero from the Kingdom of mate
While riding his stallion (it must have been fate)
Bumped into the princess that very same night
Their eyes met other - "twas love at first sight

As is the case with all fairy tales
There's a mean wicked witch casting horrible
spells
To make everyone's life a complete misery
And this tale is no exception as you will soon
see

Wicked witch Leanne - the horrible hag
In her former years was a bit of a slag

She wanted Prince Perry for her very own
Complete with his spa, yacht and of course
stately home.

Now the wicked witch - the mean ugly cow
Tricked our poor Jo into a chastity vow
With spiteful words Leanne said if it's not true
love you'll fall down dead

Now this is where the plot gets thicker and poor
Jo's luck starts looking sicker
Witchy hired two con men
To make Jo think she was in love with them

The Earl of Prattsville - Dean to his mates
His tyrannical ways were a terrible trait
He'd snarl and he'd spit his language was crude
And his sexual habits were very rude

The Duke of Wankerstown was called Dick
Not too good looking and not very quick
He spoke with a lisp and walked with a limp
And moonlighted at weekends as the
neighbourhood pimp

Leanne using her potions created magic
This part is sad and very tragic
She cast a spell so Perry would misbehave
And turned him into her sexual slave

Jo was heartbroken she was torn in two
She cried and cried she didn't know what to do
She thought that her prince had eloped with
Leanne
She thought she had lost him forever her
wonderful man

The Duke and the Earl tried to soften the blow
But their intentions were warped as you all
know
To take fair Jo and her body use
In a warped display of sexual abuse

In a flash of light two fairy goddesses appear
and made their opinion very clear
Goddess number one - called Claire
Said buck up Jo and listen here
Take your Prince and shag him rotten
Those other creeps will soon be forgotten

While goddess two the one called Vic
Said c'mon Jo make it quick
Drop your drawers and spread em wide
It will be the best thing you've ever tried

True love it seems did prevail
And now it's time to end this tale
But first we must tie up loose ends

And tell you what happened to our friends

Leanne took a fancy to Dick and Dean
Their antics together were quite obscene
They embarked on a non stop shag fest
But died in the process and were soon laid to
rest

As for Perry and Jo their love making continued
As they frolicked and cavorted around in the
nude
Their United Kingdom's were filled with
laughter
And the couple lived happily ever after

Bullshit

Why can't people stick to facts
Rather than talking lots of crap.
Making out that their life is fun and frolics
When it's really a pile of bollocks

They're bragging and shouting it out
I just wish that they'd get caught out
Pretending they're something there not
when it's really a a load of old rot

Talking about people they've known and about
the designer stuff they once owned,
Twisting and distorting the truth.
About things that they did in their youth

They probably believe their own nonsense
And have no concept of conscience
But no matter how much they embellish it
It will be forever and always bullshit

I want to write a poem

I want to write a poem
But I dont know what to write
And I'm lying here just pondering keeping me
awake at night

I want the words to flow
I hope it all makes sense
But this poem is nonsensical
And I'm losing confidence

A poem for my unborn

I never got to hold you hand
Or see your tiny smile
I never got to hear your voice
Or sit with you a while

I never got to hold you close
Or whisper I love you so
I never got to say your name
It was time to let you go

You will forever be with me
Tucked safely in my heart
You were once a part of me
So we will never be apart

The End

Ding dong let's rejoice
Raise your hands and make some noise

It's time to celebrate
The end has come and not too late

So thank you for coming I hope you had fun
Although this may not be for everyone

I hope that you smiled, maybe laughed or cried
Was it good or bad? Only you can decide.

I'm sorry for the rudeness I can't help myself
And if it's too much just leave it on the shelf